YOUR KNOWLEDGE HAS VALUE

- We will publish your bachelor's and master's thesis, essays and papers

- Your own eBook and book - sold worldwide in all relevant shops

- Earn money with each sale

Upload your text at www.GRIN.com
and publish for free

Bibliographic information published by the German National Library:

The German National Library lists this publication in the National Bibliography; detailed bibliographic data are available on the Internet at http://dnb.dnb.de .

This book is copyright material and must not be copied, reproduced, transferred, distributed, leased, licensed or publicly performed or used in any way except as specifically permitted in writing by the publishers, as allowed under the terms and conditions under which it was purchased or as strictly permitted by applicable copyright law. Any unauthorized distribution or use of this text may be a direct infringement of the author s and publisher s rights and those responsible may be liable in law accordingly.

Imprint:

Copyright © 2019 GRIN Verlag
Print and binding: Books on Demand GmbH, Norderstedt Germany
ISBN: 9783668956001

This book at GRIN:

https://www.grin.com/document/471430

David Sidikie Yambasu

"Quantum Shift in the Global Brain". Book Review

GRIN Verlag

GRIN - Your knowledge has value

Since its foundation in 1998, GRIN has specialized in publishing academic texts by students, college teachers and other academics as e-book and printed book. The website www.grin.com is an ideal platform for presenting term papers, final papers, scientific essays, dissertations and specialist books.

Visit us on the internet:

http://www.grin.com/

http://www.facebook.com/grincom

http://www.twitter.com/grin_com

DAVID SIDIKIE YAMBASU

"SEMINAR INTERNATIONAL DEVELOPMENT II"
QUANTUM SHIFT IN THE GLOBAL BRAIN

Student's Profile
A postgraduate student on a doctorate program in Project Management Living in Sierra Leone, West Africa

ATLANTIC INTERNATIONAL UNIVERSITY
HONOLULU, HAWAI
WINTER 2019

Table of Contents

Introduction 3

General analysis and Discussions......................... 5

Conclusions 9

Statement about Like or Dislike..........................10

General Recommendations 11

Bibliography 12

INTRODUCTION

> *"Change is no longer mere theory ... no longer merely an option, it is a reality, an imperative of our survival."* **Ervin Laszlo (2008)**

This piece of work clearly puts together a report on Ervin Laszlo's scientific research and explanation in a framework and his sense of " oneness." As a philosopher of science, Laszlo uses quantum physics to present a holistic perspective of the as it were " the emerging new world. " He presents people as change agents anchoring his argument on the effects of peoples activities on nature. In his change and shift discourse, Laszlo presents two approaches: That of " Business as usual " and that of " Timely Transformation". In his critical reasoning of what he has described as " macroshift" Laszlo presents four phases of the shift process: The Trigger Phase, The Transformation Phase, The critical / chaotic phase where he lays emphasis on the three Cs (Communication, consciousness and connections) and the breakdown phase .

This narrative focuses on evolutions; in his words, Laszlo says "... We are on the threshold of a new stage of social, spiritual and cultural evolution..." (p.133) He presents a fine blend of two narratives ; a research report and his experience both focusing on shifts and changes : " reality transformation." He also insists that these shifts 'are under our feet ' and hence his discourse on the evolution of sub cultures and the subsequent emerging changes in the values, ethics, cultures with their attendant shifts. His arguments are metaphysical, theological with ethical implications. He also presents the cosmic plenum as the new fundamental concept of reality.

Laszlo presents his contribution especially to that of the Akasbic Field (p153). He presents it in three parts: part one ; " *Our Changing world,*" focuses on the macroshift which is a narrative that emphasises, living with change , demanding an understanding of that change process if we do not wish to degenerate into crisis. Part two " *Understanding our changing world in map;*" is a theoretical argument of the paradigm shift. It discusses the concept of reality as it interfaces with the outcomes of scientific research in the change trajectory.

Part three can be summarized as a narrative of *"The new map of reality,"* In this section, Laszlo blends experience with theory to contribute to innovation resulting from scientific insights which suggests options for resilience, well being and human survival.

Laszlo prescribes 10 approaches to the shift trajectory which others have referred to as " Laszlo's 10 commandments" which he highlights in chapter fifteen *captioned as 'manifesto on planetary consciousness' (p.133).* These prescriptions in my opinion, are begging for solidarity among individuals and nations thus underpinning the argument of his theory of " Oneness" painting the picture of a global family where people live ways that others may live while respecting life and safeguarding right to life. The prescriptions as it were, make room for analysing juxtaposing concepts such as; extensive growth versus intensive growth, isolation versus connection. Laszlo's vision about change or the quantum shift, requires inner growth.

I find the closing annex as a "new story' in the discuss of communications beyond the grave as well as that of the Instrumental Transcommunication (ITC) as it relates to that of the macroshift. In trying to present this ground breaking field, Laszlo tries to present a logical narrative of his experience and its explanations so that his readers can buy his story. This evolution story of a high level of communication is indeed ground breaking. As an innovative approach, Laszlo presents the Club of Budapest in chapter fourteen, which he founded as a think tank focusing on 'soft factors' including values, expectations, worldviews, state of minds and consciousness (p.130).

Communicating beyond the grave is a new scientific study for confirming faith in the after life .(p.155). It is worth noting that to date there are still a range of controlled experiments conducted with the aim of justifying or broadening the debate that there is an afterlife (p.158).

As a prolific writer, Laszlo has published 83 books with copies available in 21 languages. He is a winner of two Nobel Peace Prizes, chancellor designate of the GlobalShift University and president of the international think tanks of Budapest. This is an interesting read with a mixture of philosophy, science, global world views, some theology and experience sharing.

GENERAL ANALYSIS AND DISCUSSIONS

Based on his scientific analysis, Laszlo presents a rather gloomy picture of planet earth and humanity. He describes the globe as on that is experiencing dual shifts these being : a shift in nature and that of science through technological advancements put in his words ; " the reality revolution." These shifts are bound to cause a sudden and fundamental transformation in the relationship of the 6.5 billion people living on the globe.

This is a narrative of a shifting nature of human beings, as they interface with each other irrespective of the varying levels and social capital. This piece of work argues with an open mind the concept of the reality revolution as an opportunity of either ending the old era of as the beginning of a new cycle of life which maybe sustainable in the given perspective of conscious shifts in the sub-cultures, ethics and values in the spirit of " *oneness.*'

Laszlo argues that these emerging perspectives are characterised by shocks and surprises. In his opinion, instead of the changing realities due to the shift in nature and science, rather it is the surprises of individuals resulting from internalised shifts. He uses Kenneth Boulding's submission (p.1) to support his argument that " the only thing we should not be surprised at is being surprised." This is quite philosophical and does leave room for further discussion, which is beyond the scope of this general analysis. In this discourse, Laszlo uses a tripartite analogy in presenting the reality shift. He presents the varying outcomes of how we relate to each other, how we relate to nature and how we relate to the cosmos as possible reasons for the shock and surprises which begs for the quantum shift. This reality transformation begs the question as to whether it must continue to be " Business as usual" or whether ' reality shift' should in effect lead to a macroshift? If the latter is the case, it creates room for understanding that this new era of scientific reality, business will not be as usual.

Laszlo presents concrete justifications to convince his readers that indeed the world is changing and this resonates with the present scientific explanations of the effects of climate change on nature and its effects on the human race. Among the examples presented are the absence of snow on the top of mount Kilimanjaro and that of the Russians celebrating on New Year's Eve in the former Red square without a trace of ice and snow.

He extends the transformations running in the spheres of ecology, social, political and culture. This reality transformation he asserts, has potentials of resulting into a catastrophe on planet earth (the chaos phase of reality transformation). He insists that :

> "... Change is no longer mere theory... no longer merely an option, it is a reality, an imperative of survival." (Ervin Laszlo,2008)

Laszlo further describes change within quantum shifts as radical and not linear. These shifts at terminal points can either breakdown or bifurcate using the analogy of the galaxy of stars which grow and go into extinction marking the end of an old generation as well as beginning a of a new era. However, Laszlo holds the view that in the middle of the realty transformation, like other species, the human species is not likely to degenerate to extinction. This is so because of the available adaptation options provided by the advancing technological outputs and the scientific coping backups. He validates this assertion with the argument of our interconnectedness and closeness to the earth as well as our cosmos linkage in the spiritual realm also underscoring the effects of our " oneness."

Laszlo continue his argument by prescribing ten approaches towards effective management of the Macroshift or the outcomes of the emerging evolution which other commentators have referred to as " Laszlo's 10 commandments." This it would seem as a call for a new way of life or a manifesto of planetary consciousness or simply put ' a new direction' of the human family. In his prescriptions, he guards against in effective coping with the present and future shocks as the outcomes of these shocks are bound to influence our future and the future of our children and grandchildren (p.133). He urges us to create the framework for building a peaceful and cooperative global society. A further analysis of the global quantum shift shows the inequality among the human community. Laszlo paints a picture of a world where millions of people are without work, millions are being exploited by poor wages, millions are forced into helplessness and poverty. He further argues that the gap between the rich and poor nations as well as that between rich poor people within nations is great and still growing (p.134). Laszlo reflects on today's patterns of actions, which he describes as appalling.

Laszlo argues that attempting to solve the world's problems from militarization to ecology through what it takes to achieve sustainable development should not be a short –term problem solving approach; instead, it must beyond reasoning and extended to include the power of love, compassion and solidarity. Similarly, striving for a global and peaceful co-existence should be the urge in the changing life styles and in the styles of work.

This new way of immersing into the challenges of the evolution will spur us into deeper analysis of the problems which beds for a rethink which will be harnessed as opportunities and a global call to action . This call to action is anchored in our own creativity as a result of today's economic, social and technological environment demanding us to cope with it. This will help the human family live together peacefully, cooperatively with reciprocity of benefits. Laszlo affirms the need for the existing differences in the human community in terms of age, sex, colour, personality or creed. It is this diversity that provides for complementarity among each other which does allow growth and evolution. Based on the realities and demands of the diversity debate, Laszlo concludes that if this were not the case, it would mean that today's world is endangered by few cultures and civilisations which continue to overshadow the others.

Therefore, Laszlo argues that a critical challenge would be that of sustaining diversity. This he states would require international and intercultural contacts while respecting each other's differences, beliefs, life styles and ambitions. This approach he further argues, calls for the recognition of equal values and dignity of all peoples and cultures; a human community, where people have right to their own space, actively working in solidarity with each other (p.136).

Laszlo invites the human family to become responsible actors in a holistic sense instead of safeguarding individual rights. This requires a shift towards a peaceful and cooperative human family that is non-violent and responsible socially, economically, politically and culturally. In sum therefore, Laszlo calls the human family to planetary consciousness. Every member of the human community is urged to evolve their consciousness to the planetary dimension.

As an innovative approach, Laszlo presents the Club of Budapest in chapter fourteen, which he founded as a think tank focusing on 'soft factors' including values, expectations, worldviews, state of minds and consciousness (p.130). As a mission for the club he is very clear on what the club should engage in. Among what could be describe as terms of references for the club of Budapest were: serving as it were, " a factory" for the production of positive change agents who will stimulate the radical change process in both public and private institutions. This expectation led to the creation of the Global Shift University (p.140). It also attracted like-minded institutions and organizations thus leading to the formation and active transformational engagements of the civilization alliance, the World Wisdom Alliance, the world wisdom council and the international survey of Emerging Cultures. All of these systems approach to managing the global shift with its shocks and surprises, gear towards offering doable guidelines for the human community to effectively interface with the 'new' planetary civilization especially at a time when religious doctrines have now lost their roles with the advent of science.

As a ground breaking filed, Laszlo concludes his book on a very controversial note of science and experience on the theme of After Death Communication (

ADC) which he presents hypothetically. He uses asumptios and advances possible scientific explanations of possibilities of such communications after death . which may occur in dreams. An opposing debate from a scientific and anthropological perspective can hold a view according to Laszlo that modern technology can also induce after death communications through the use of the " sensory desensitization and reprocessing " techniques. This discourse has generated interests in the " afterlife" debate. It has also stimulated further scientific research in this filed including those of David Fontano, Anabela Cardoso and others (p.159). I suggest that we save the outcomes and findings of these scientific investigations for other book reviews.

CONCLUSIONS

In my opinion , Laszlo's approach to the global world view or map though philosophical, thus add to body of knowledge in the on going debate of globalization. This fine blend of metaphysical theology, quantum physics and philosophy does fit into the contemporary debate of globalization and its effects on world economy, politics, technological advancements, climate change, ecology and the emerging sub cultures. His practical us of the Club of Budapest could be likened to an action research which seeks to understand the problem(s), make suggestions for long term problem solving and reviewing the outcomes. His peace of work is consistent with that of attempting to identify the existing problems, gather evidence, contribute to knowledge through publications of visual materials, reports and books to raise awareness on the evolving situations which he often refers to sub-cultures .

I find the closing annex as a "new story' in the discuss of communications beyond the grave as well as that of the Instrumental Transcommunication (ITC) as it relates to that of the macroshift.. This debate will continue among scientists and theologians although Laszlo argues that religious doctrines have now lost their roles with the advent of science.

Do I like or dislike the book?

As a development practitioner, I like the book. It suggest critical approaches to both long term and short term problem solving beginning with the root cause identification. Although written over a decade ago, its arguments resonate with the current discuss about climate change, globalisation, emerging sub-cultures across the globe.

The practical use of the Club of Budapest with prescribed roles and responsibilities of members and well written out a " How –to-guide, is an account of a practical experience sharing as a learning opportunity for practitioners in the fields of development, research and management. I will refer to part three of he book as a" How –To Guide " for action planning and effective implementation of initiatives. (Pp.127-151).

I particularly like his writing style as he pays greater attention to his descriptions, analysis, explanations and practical examples. Take his 'communications beyond the grave' for instance; he explores the question does it occur? He tries to find out to whom, why and when making room for diverse views although he now spirals down to a scientific explanation of " sensory desensitization and reprocessing techniques" as a way of explaining after-death communication. In a way, he tries to convince his readers into buying his submission that the new scientific reality can indeed change the human family and the global village.

Although I strongly agree with most of his arguments, I am of the view that moral theologians will disagree with Laszlo's assertion that " religious doctrines have now lost their roles with the advent of science" especially in modern times when religion as a sub-culture, is emerging as a political and economic commodity. This is however another debate for perhaps another forum.

General Recommendations

To be able to critically engage in the contemporary discourse about climate change and globalisation, Laszlo's piece of work on " Quantum Shift in the Global Brain" (2008) is a good read and reference material. I therefore recommend it to readers with multidisciplinary fields of interests.

It is a indeed a good read !

Bibliography

Laszlo, E. (2008) Quantum Shift in the Global Brain: How the New Scientific Reality Can Change us and our world. Inner Traditions. Rochester, Vermont

YOUR KNOWLEDGE HAS VALUE

- We will publish your bachelor's and master's thesis, essays and papers

- Your own eBook and book - sold worldwide in all relevant shops

- Earn money with each sale

Upload your text at www.GRIN.com and publish for free